Give Me Back My Creativity

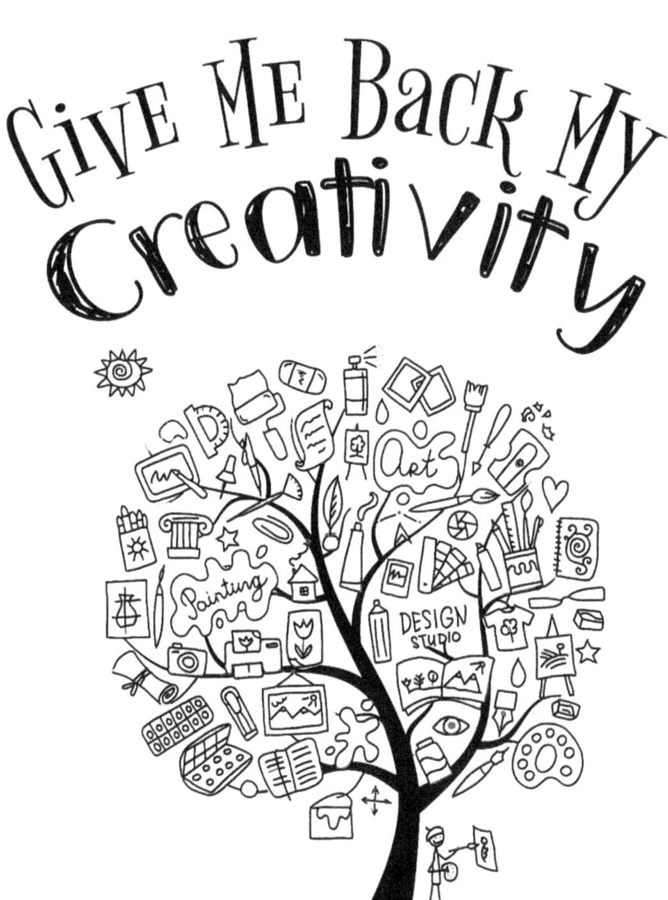

A Weekly Planner
from the author of *Give Me Back My Crayons*

JoAnn Nocera

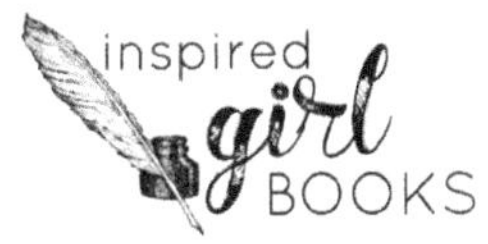

Give Me Back My Creativity: A Weekly Planner from the author of Give Me Back My Crayons
Published by Inspired Girl Books
821 Belmar Plaza, Unit 5 Belmar, NJ 07719
www.inspiredgirlbooks.com

Inspired Girl Books is honored to bring forth books with heart and stories that matter. We are proud to offer this book to our readers; the story, the experiences, and the words are the author's alone.

This book is written as a source of information only. The information contained in this book should by no means be considered a substitute for the advice of a qualified medical professional, who should always be consulted before beginning any new diet, exercise, or other health program and before taking any dietary supplements or other medications.

The author and publisher do not assume and hereby disclaim any liability in connection with the use of the information contained in this book.

Products, pictures, trademarks, and trademark names are used throughout this book to describe and inform the reader about various proprietary products that are owned by third parties. No endorsement of the information contained in this book is given by the owners of such products and trademarks, and no endorsement is implied by the inclusion of products, pictures, or trademarks in this book.

© 2020 JoAnn Nocera
All rights reserved. No portion of this book may be reproduced in any form without permission from the publisher, except as permitted by U.S. copyright law. For permissions contact: help@inspiredgirlbooks.com

ISBN: 978-0-578-68830-5
Cover and interior design by Roseanna White Designs
Illustrations from Shutterstock

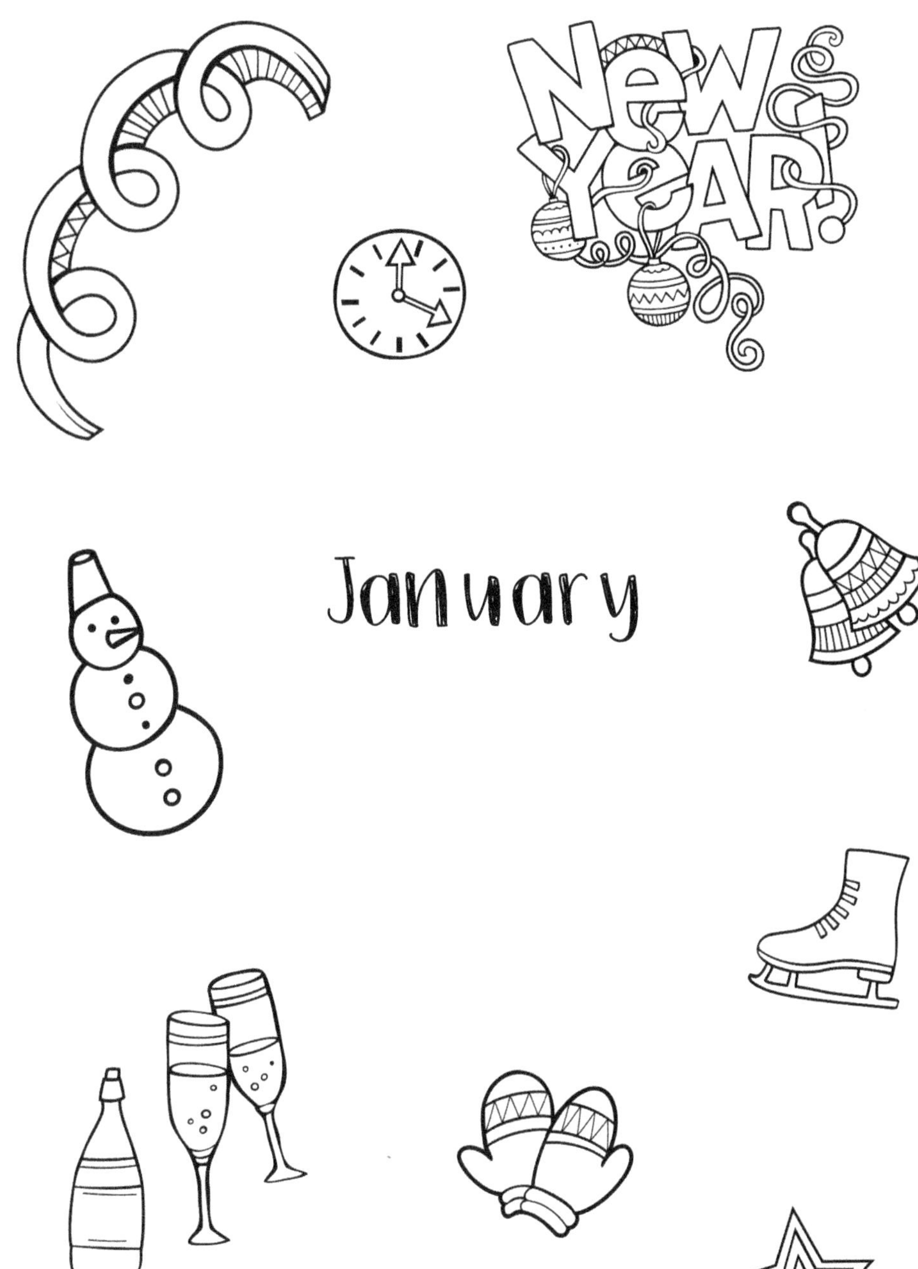

January

The Universe buries
strange jewels
deep within us all,
and then stands back
to see if we
can find them.

~ Elizabeth Gilbert

January

Week of

Sunday

Monday

Tuesday

Wednesday

Thursday

Friday

Saturday

Write It Out...

New Year...New You!

Write 3 goals for yourself for the month. Begin slow and don't overwhelm yourself in getting them accomplished tomorrow.

January

Week of ____________

Sunday

Monday

Tuesday

Wednesday

Thursday

Friday

Saturday

Mindful Reflection

If I have to let go of three things in my life
what would they be...

Reflect on your life and all the "things" that we fill it with.
Which "things" can you live without?
Why are they not important anymore?

January

Week of

Sunday

Monday

Tuesday

Wednesday

Thursday

Friday

Saturday

Mak er Moment

Stuffy Fluffy Sweater

Is there a sweater that is too small or you are looking to donate? Why not upcycle it into a stuffy fluffy friend?

- ◊ Draw on paper an animal or person.
- ◊ Cut it and trace it on the sweater.
- ◊ Make sure the sweater is flat so when you cut out the shape both front and back sweater are cut at the same time.
- ◊ Decorate the front and back using felt, yarn, buttons, etc
- ◊ Stitch around edges using a blanket stitch (check out the blind stitch video @ http://bit.ly/YouTubeBlanketStitch)

- ◊ Leave an opening so there is enough space to stuff with polyester fill
- ◊ Stitch closed the opening

Cuddle up with your stuffy fluffy. We all need a hug!

#givemebackmycrayonsJanuary

January

Week of ____________

Sunday

Monday

Tuesday

Wednesday

Thursday

Friday

Saturday

Photo / Artwork Picture

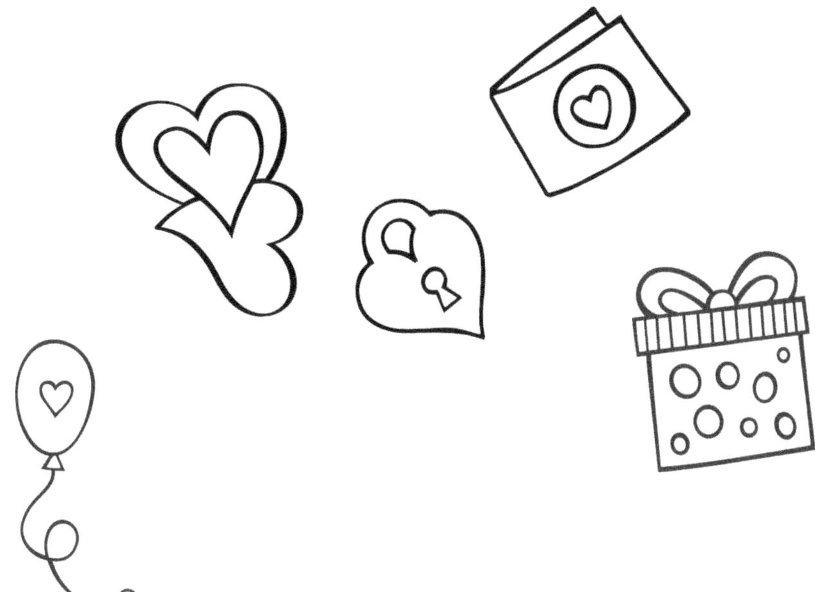

February

Speak
little,
do
much.

~ Benjamin
Franklin

February

Week of ____________

Sunday

Monday

Tuesday

Wednesday

Thursday

Friday

Saturday

Write It Out...

What do I wish more people knew about me?

Write about the first person you fell in love with
or the first thing you truly loved.

February

Week of ____________

Sunday

Monday

Tuesday

Wednesday

Thursday

Friday

Saturday

Mindful Reflection

Look up!

Study the moon this month and how it casts shadows.
Do you see any stars? The night sky is usually full of surprises.

February

Week of ____________

Sunday

Monday

Tuesday

Wednesday

Thursday

Friday

Saturday

Mak er Moment

Pick 5 Different Pieces of Music!

Play each song and dance!
Dance like no one is watching.
Move your body freely and any way you want.
Just Dance!!!!

Feel your body move differently to the wide array of songs.
Try different genres of songs, Jazz, Classical, Rap, Country, etc.

#givemebackmycrayonsFebruary

February

Week of

Sunday

Monday

Tuesday

Wednesday

Thursday

Friday

Saturday

Photo / Artwork Picture

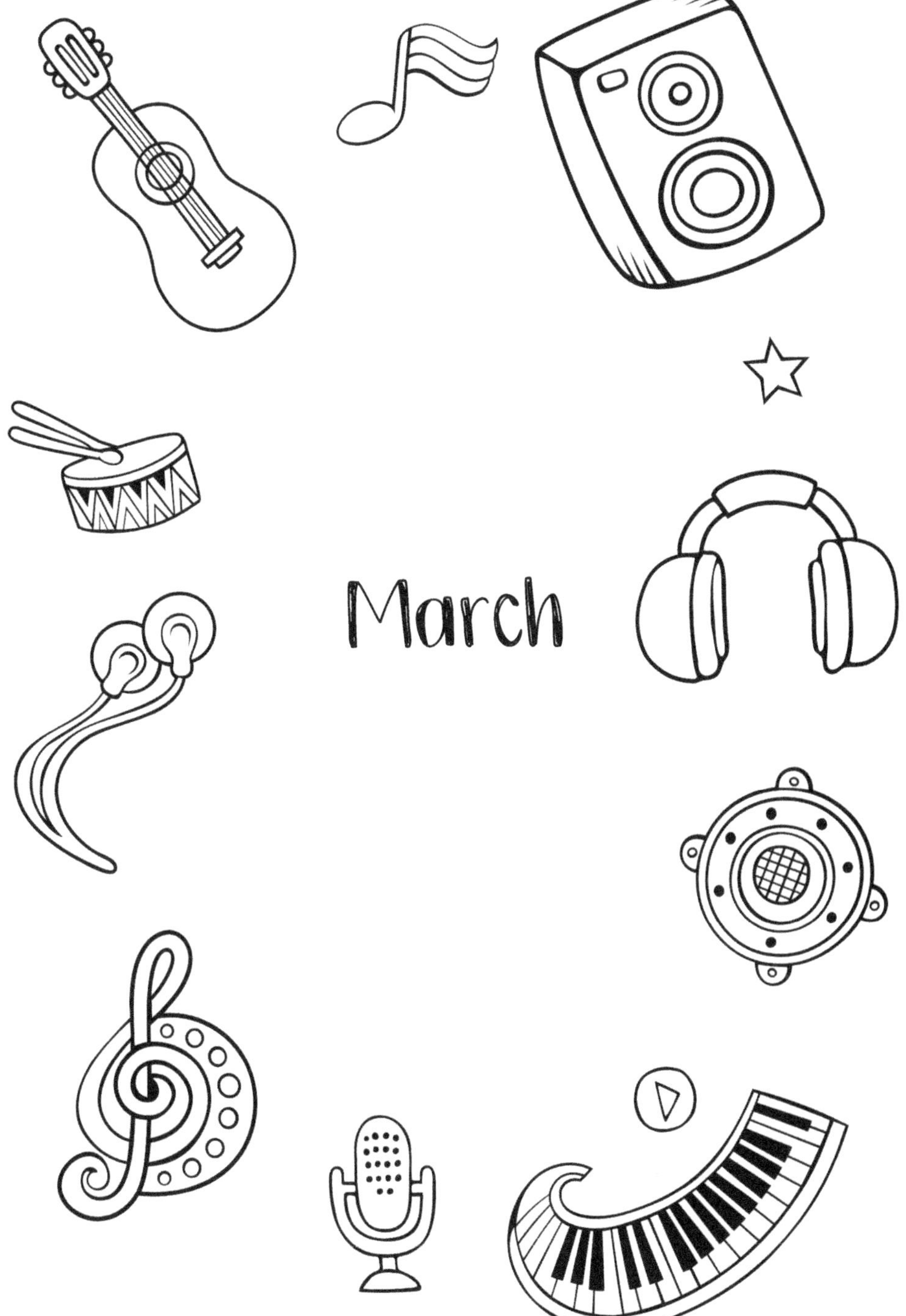
March

CREATIVITY
is allowing yourself
to make mistakes.
ART
is knowing
which ones to keep.

~Scott Adams

March

Week of ____________

Sunday

Monday

Tuesday

Wednesday

Thursday

Friday

Saturday

Write It Out...

"Writing is your heart coming down your arms into your fingers and onto the paper."

Take some time with pencil, pen and paper and just write down whatever comes into your mind. Don't worry about spelling or perfect grammar/punctuation. Be free to write whatever is in your heart.

March

Week of ____________

Sunday

Monday

Tuesday

Wednesday

Thursday

Friday

Saturday

Mindful Reflection

March to a Healthy Beat

Reflect on your past week and write down the foods you have given your body. Think about if they provided nutrition. Place importance on including more vegetables and fruits into your meals as they provide nourishment for the mind and body.

Write a healthy meal plan for the month.

March

Week of ______

Sunday

Monday

Tuesday

Wednesday

Thursday

Friday

Saturday

Maker Moment

Scrabble is a great way to get the mind thinking creatively.

Pick up 15 letters of your choice and try to make
as many words using these pieces.
Try to use those words to create a picture,
piece of writing or a structure out of legos or playdough.
See where your creative mind takes you!

#givemebackmycrayonsMarch

March

Week of

Sunday

Monday

Tuesday

Wednesday

Thursday

Friday

Saturday

Photo / Artwork Picture

April

They're only
CRAYONS.
You didn't fear them
in kindergarten.
Why fear them
now?

~ Hugh MacLeod

April

Week of ____________

Sunday

Monday

Tuesday

Wednesday

Thursday

Friday

Saturday

Write It Out...

What is your favorite tree?

Give three reasons why you like it so much.

April

Week of

Sunday

Monday

Tuesday

Wednesday

Thursday

Friday

Saturday

Mindful Reflection

Coloring

Use your crayons to create a calming and meditative session with the picture below:

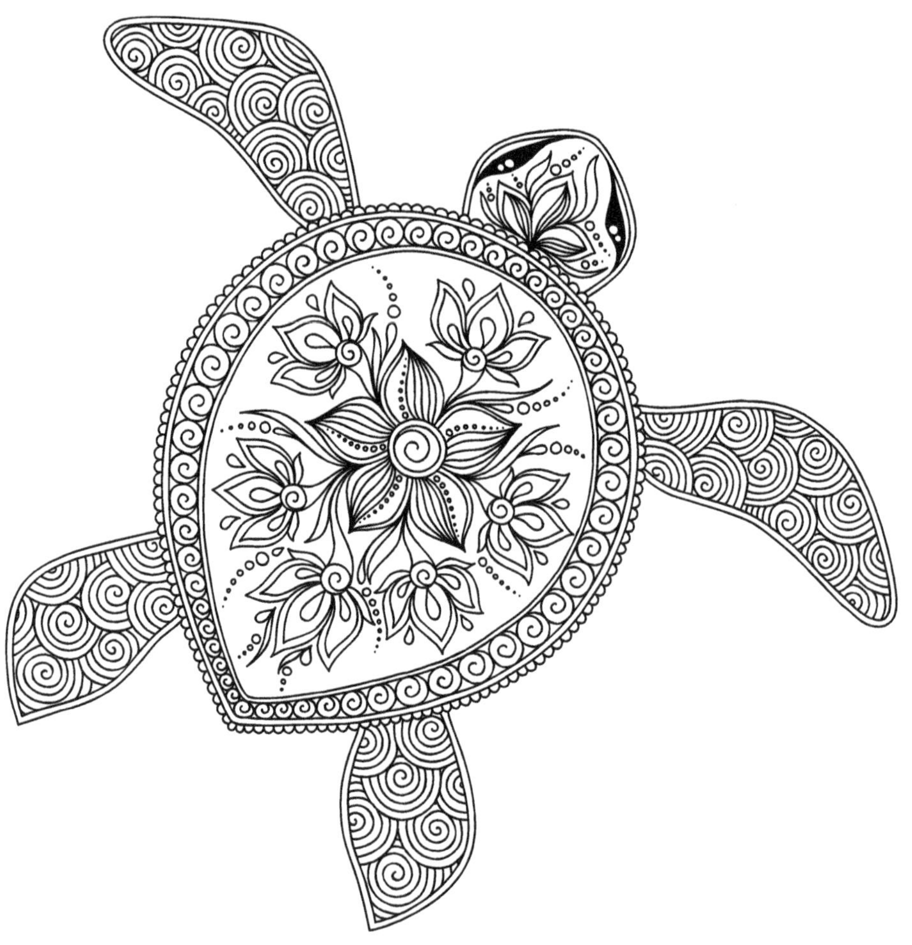

April

Week of ______

Sunday

Monday

Tuesday

Wednesday

Thursday

Friday

Saturday

Mak er Moment

Rock Weaving

- ◊ Find a large rock
- ◊ Pick a color yarn color yarn to wrap the rock in vertical lines around the rock leave some space between each line
- ◊ Use a plastic needle to thread a different color yarn.
- ◊ Weave the colored yarn (over and under each vertical strand)
- ◊ When you reach the end weave back the way you came.
- ◊ Change the needle to a different color or fancy yard to create a 3D effect
- ◊ Use your imagination.

#givemebackmycrayonsApril

April

Week of

Sunday

Monday

Tuesday

Wednesday

Thursday

Friday

Saturday

Photo / Artwork Picture

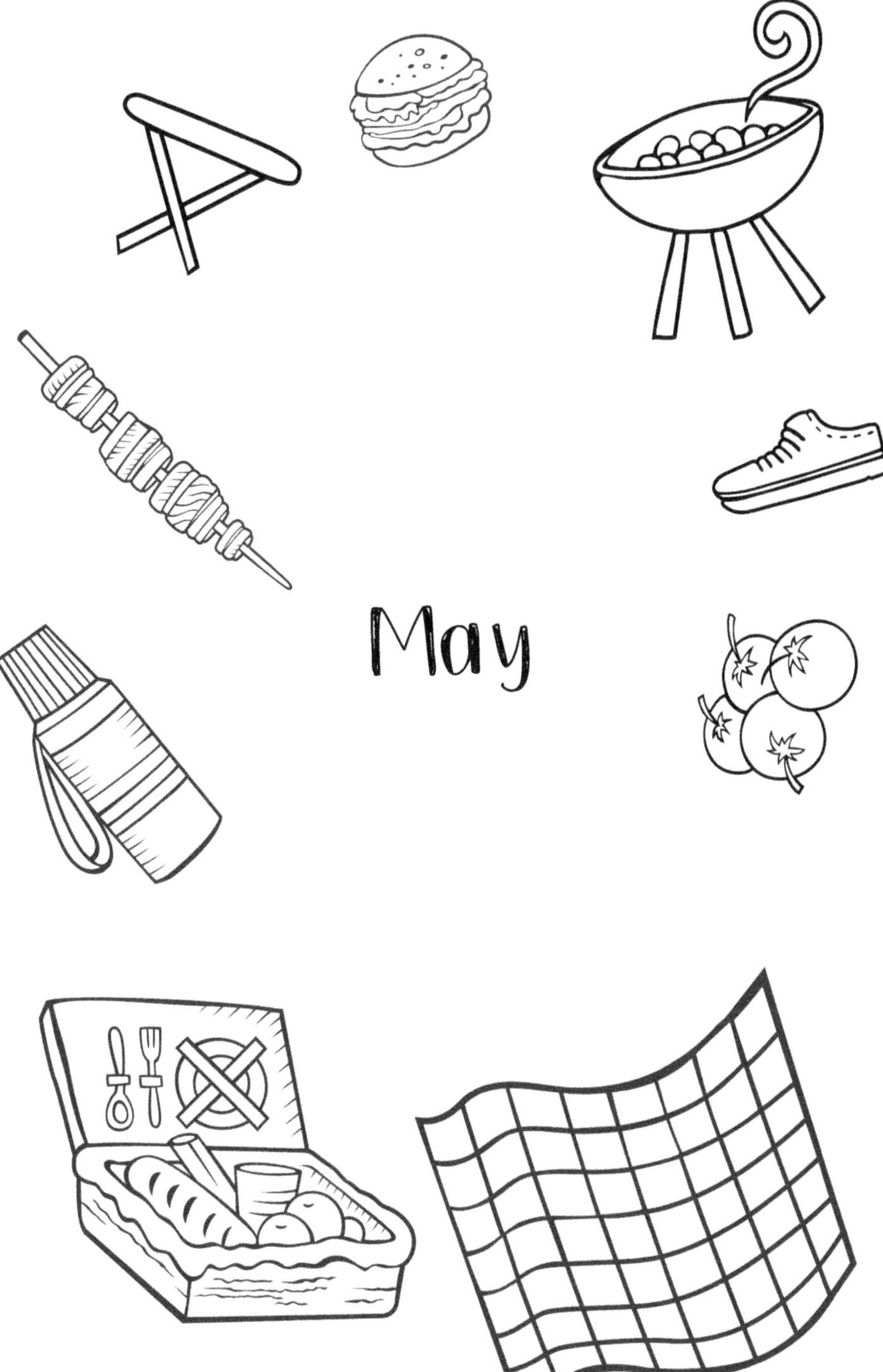
May

You can't use up
creativity,
the more you
use,
the more you
have.

- Maya Angelou

May

Week of ____________

Sunday

Monday

Tuesday

Wednesday

Thursday

Friday

Saturday

Write It Out...

I like to spend my time outside...

May

Week of ____________

Sunday

Monday

Tuesday

Wednesday

Thursday

Friday

Saturday

Mindful Reflection

Sense of Touch

Turn off all distractions for 5-10 minutes

Look around for a texture or surface that is smooth or bumpy.

Notice how it feels.

Our senses, especially our sense of touch, are important as they provide us with a powerful connection to the emotional and physical well being.

Take time to massage your shoulders, neck, breathing in and out.

When washing your face and moisturizing it at night, take extra time to give your face a massage

May

Week of

Sunday

Monday

Tuesday

Wednesday

Thursday

Friday

Saturday

Mak er Moment

Create a Vision Board

- ◊ Place a picture of yourself in the middle of the board
- ◊ Collect images and things to add to it
- ◊ Don't fill every space - Keep some space open as this will be changed and things added throughout the months ahead.

Materials needed:

- ◊ Tape, glue, scissors, crayons, stickers
- ◊ Magazines, newspapers, photos,
- ◊ Quotes, affirmations, sayings, etc

#givemebackmycrayonsMay

May

Week of ______________

Sunday

Monday

Tuesday

Wednesday

Thursday

Friday

Saturday

Photo / Artwork Picture

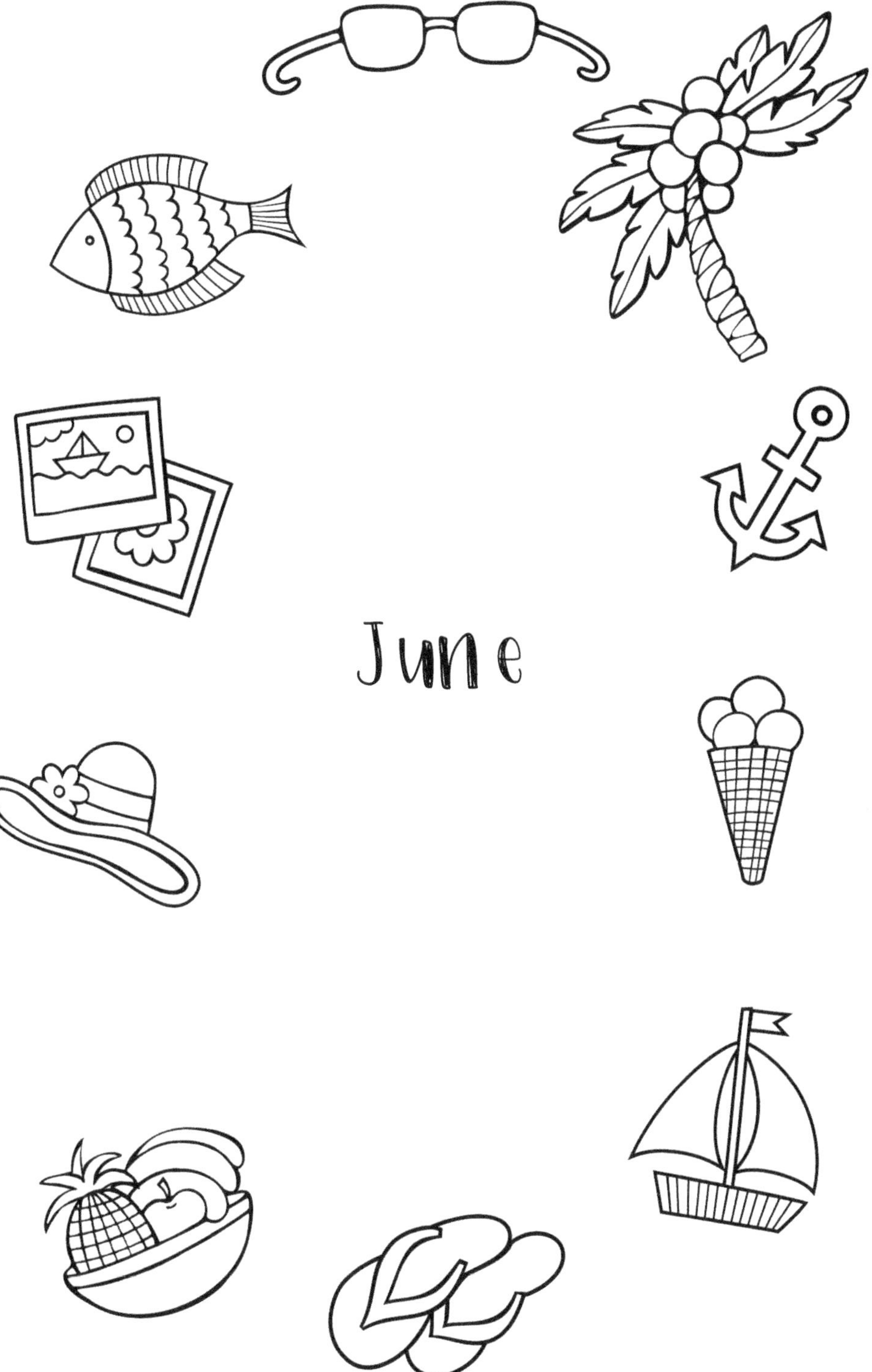

June

The artist is a
receptacle for emotions
that come from
all over the place:
from the sky, from the earth,
from a scrap of paper,
from a passing shape,
from a spider's web.

~ Pablo Picasso

June

Week of

Sunday

Monday

Tuesday

Wednesday

Thursday

Friday

Saturday

Write It Out...

I feel calm when...

Here is a list of other things that relieves my stress and places calmness and peace into my life:

June

Week of

Sunday

Monday

Tuesday

Wednesday

Thursday

Friday

Saturday

Mindful Reflection

Take a Drive

Take a scenic drive around town.

Stop at a county park or national park to walk. Breathe in the beauty that surrounds you.

Take in the sights and sounds of nature.

June

Week of

Sunday

Monday

Tuesday

Wednesday

Thursday

Friday

Saturday

Maker Moment

Create a Purse or Wallet

Duct tape comes in many sizes and colors. It can be used to create shapes and pockets by placing the sticky parts together and expanding their size and shape. Please refer to this YouTube video for techniques and you will be off to create:

https://bit.ly/YouTubeDuckTapeWallet

Materials:

◊ Duct tape (different colors and widths)

◊ Scissors

You will be ready to bring it along for vacation time.

#givemebackmycrayonsJune

June

Week of

Sunday

Monday

Tuesday

Wednesday

Thursday

Friday

Saturday

Photo / Artwork Picture

July

We travel because we need to,
because distance and difference
are the secret topic
of creativity.
When we get home,
home is still the same.
But something in our mind
has been changed
and that changes everything.

~Jonah Lehrer

July

Week of ______

Sunday

Monday

Tuesday

Wednesday

Thursday

Friday

Saturday

Exercise...

Take some time this month to...

- ◊ Go for a walk
- ◊ Ride a bike
- ◊ Running
- ◊ Swimming
- ◊ Skateboarding
- ◊ Hiking

Any activity you can think of to get your body moving.

Breath in and out releasing the anxiety and stress
that might be present at the time.

July

Week of ______

Sunday

Monday

Tuesday

Wednesday

Thursday

Friday

Saturday

Mindful Reflection

Meditate for ONE MINUTE

Take time for yourself. There is no right or wrong way to meditate.

Meditation is...focusing on an object, thought in a calm state and being present in the moment.

Increase your time each week this month.

July

Week of ________

Sunday

Monday

Tuesday

Wednesday

Thursday

Friday

Saturday

Maker Moment

Design a Boat

Draw a boat you would like to own. Add details and diagram out all the different functions it would do.

If you would like to use paper, basal wood and other materials to build a boat, you can!

Get those creative juices flowing!

#givemebackmycrayonsJuly

July

Week of

Sunday

Monday

Tuesday

Wednesday

Thursday

Friday

Saturday

Photo / Artwork Picture

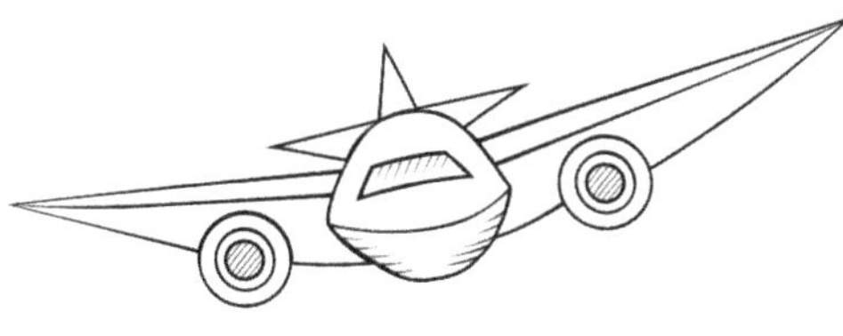

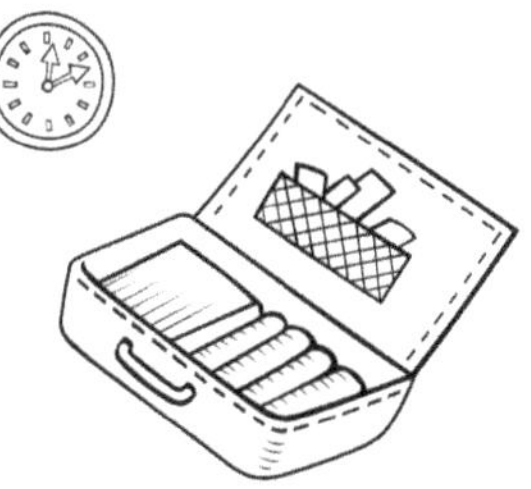

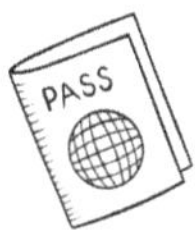

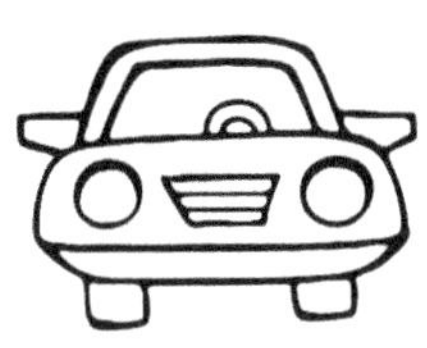

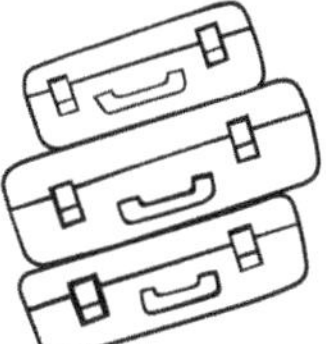

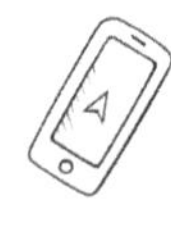

August

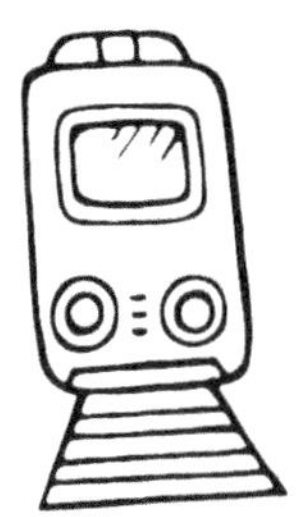

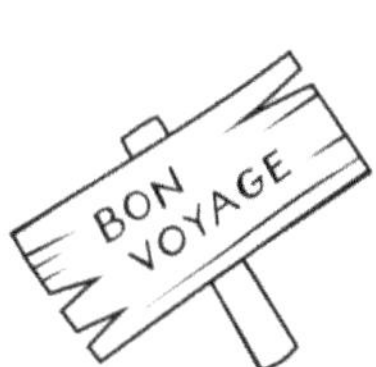

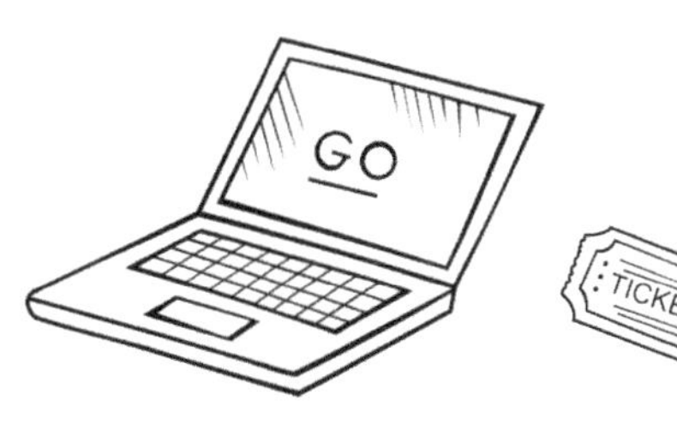

TICKET

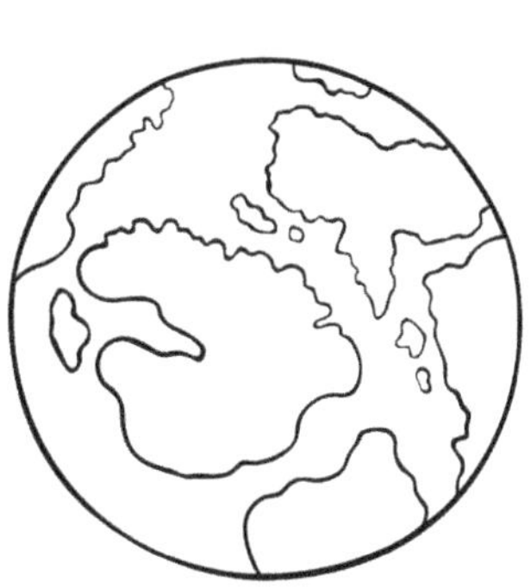

You MISS
100 percent
of the shots
you don't
TAKE.

~ Wayne Gretzky

August

Week of

Sunday

Monday

Tuesday

Wednesday

Thursday

Friday

Saturday

Write It Out...

If I had to imagine a perfect vacation,
it would include...

August

Week of

Sunday

Monday

Tuesday

Wednesday

Thursday

Friday

Saturday

Mindful Reflection

Yoga

Yoga is a perfect way to release stress or just reinforce the message of acceptance and being present.

Visit yogabasics.com for an introduction on poses. Videos are also available.

August

Week of ____________

Sunday

Monday

Tuesday

Wednesday

Thursday

Friday

Saturday

Mak er Moment

Collage

Gather pictures, photos, extra scrap papers,
words cut away from magazines, newspapers, etc.

Glue together on a piece of construction paper
and/or lightweight cardstock/cardboard for support

#givemebackmycrayonsAugust

August

Week of

Sunday

Monday

Tuesday

Wednesday

Thursday

Friday

Saturday

Photo / Artwork Picture

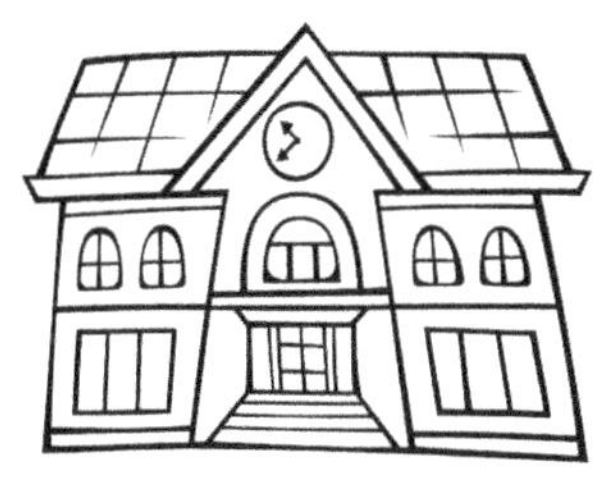
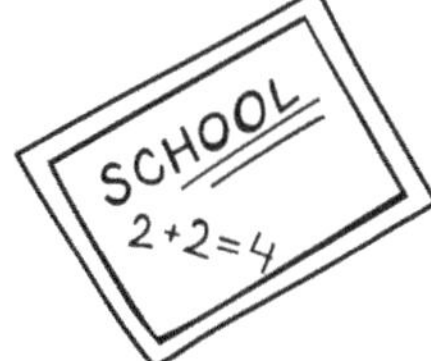
SCHOOL
2+2=4
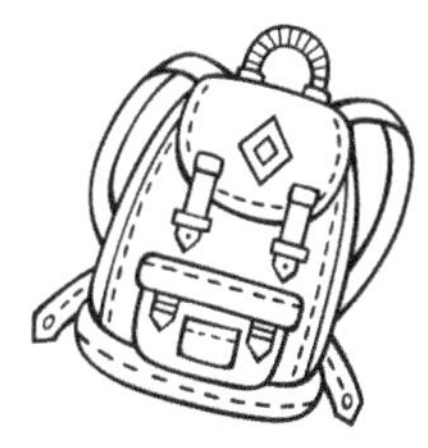
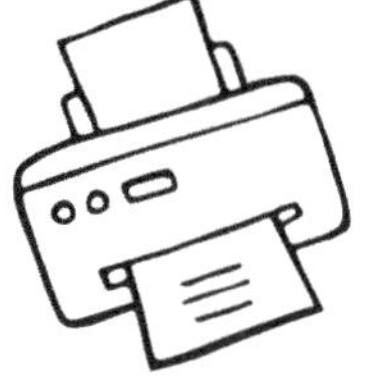
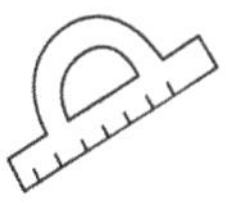
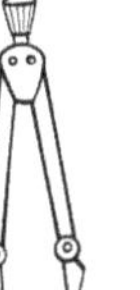
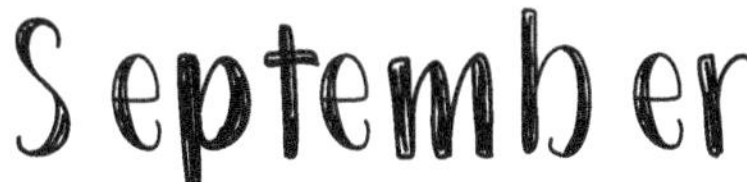
September
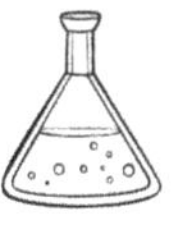
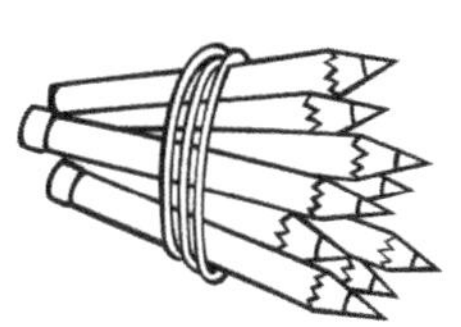
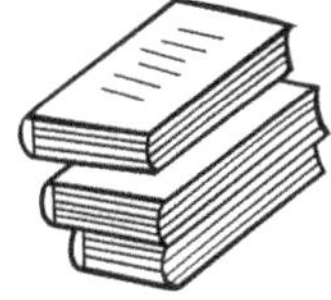
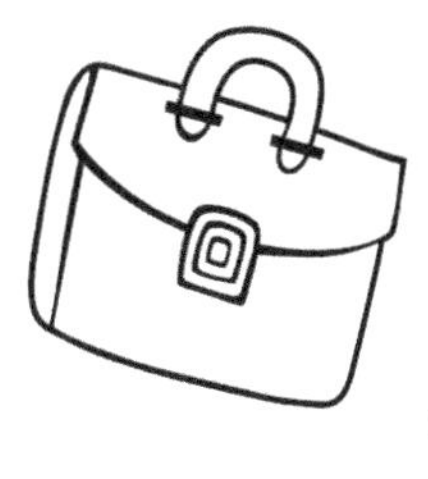
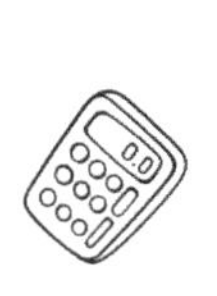
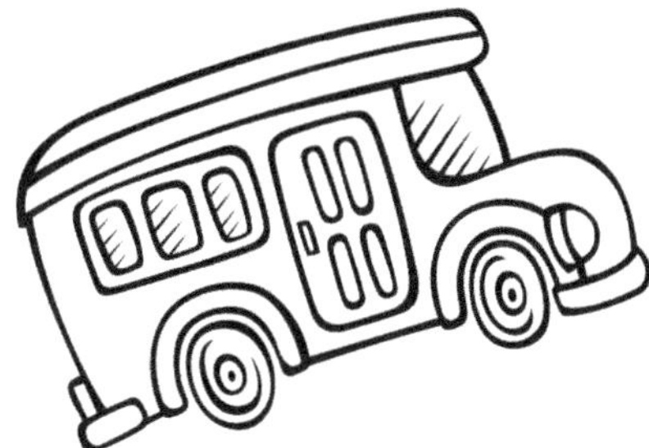

The creative instinct is

an enormous super-energy

which no single life

can consume.

~ Pearl S. Buck

September

Week of

Sunday

Monday

Tuesday

Wednesday

Thursday

Friday

Saturday

Write It Out...

Write a letter to yourself...

At 5 years old...
At 30 years old...
At 75 years old...

What would you like to remind yourself to do?
What would you say to yourself at that age?

September

Week of

Sunday

Monday

Tuesday

Wednesday

Thursday

Friday

Saturday

Mindful Reflection

Visit an Art Museum

- ◊ Pick a gallery and sit quietly
- ◊ Observe the artwork and/or sculptures
- ◊ Does any painting or artwork appeal to you? Why?
- ◊ Read the description and place yourself in that time period.
- ◊ Notice the lines, brush strokes, colors, textures etc.

September

Week of ______

Sunday

Monday

Tuesday

Wednesday

Thursday

Friday

Saturday

Mak er Moment

Stain-Glass Window

Materials:

- ◊ Black construction paper
- ◊ Colored tissue paper

Create a stained-glass window using different colored pieces of tissue paper. Outline the shapes and figures with cut up strips of black construction paper. Use straight lines, curved lines, all kinds of shapes.

#givemebackmycrayonsSeptember

September

Week of ______

Sunday

Monday

Tuesday

Wednesday

Thursday

Friday

Saturday

Photo / Artwork Picture

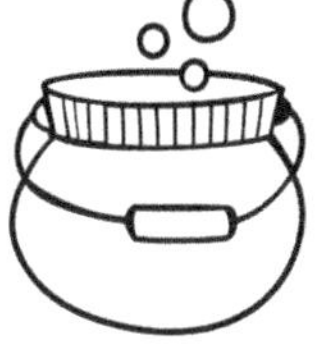

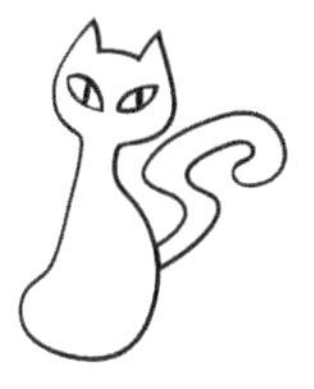

BOO

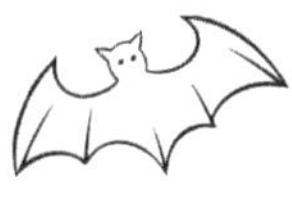

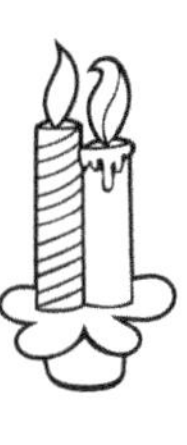

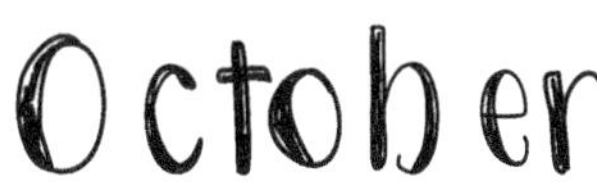
October

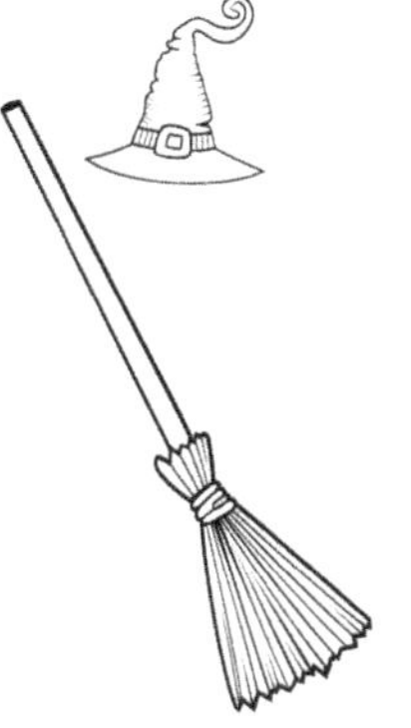

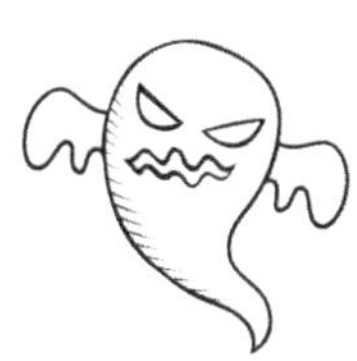

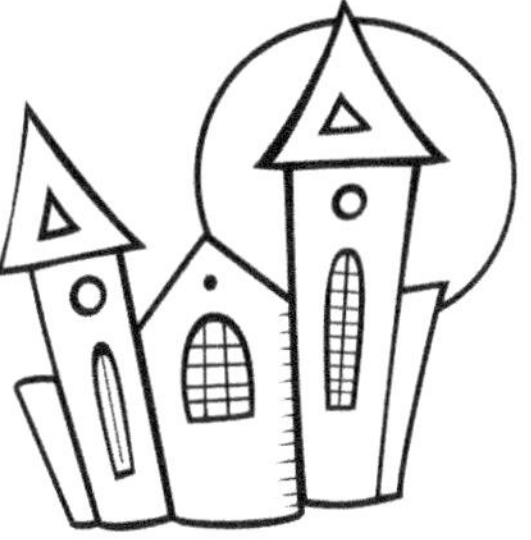

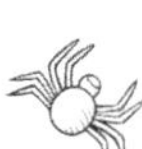

It took me a whole lifetime to paint like a child.

~ Pablo Picasso

October

Week of ______

Sunday

Monday

Tuesday

Wednesday

Thursday

Friday

Saturday

Write It Out...

What frightens me the most is...

October

Week of ____________

Sunday

Monday

Tuesday

Wednesday

Thursday

Friday

Saturday

Mindful Reflection

Create Your Own Mantra

"A mantra can be a word, a syllable, a phrase or a sound that is repeated several times as a way to help you connect and feel the energy within and around you." ~ Sherianna Boyle, author of *Mantras Made Easy: Mantras for Happiness, Peace, Prosperity and More*

Breathe in one to two words
Breathe out the rest of the words

Ex: Breathe in "I LOVE"
Breathe out "BEING ME"

October

Week of

Sunday

Monday

Tuesday

Wednesday

Thursday

Friday

Saturday

Mak er Moment

Design a Music Album Cover

Imagine if you could listen to the music and design a new cover for your favorite artist. Listen and move your pen, marker, pencil to where it feels the sounds, rhythm and patterns. Add in details using crayons, paints, colored markers, etc.

#givemebackmycrayonsOctober

October

Week of

Sunday

Monday

Tuesday

Wednesday

Thursday

Friday

Saturday

Photo / Artwork Picture

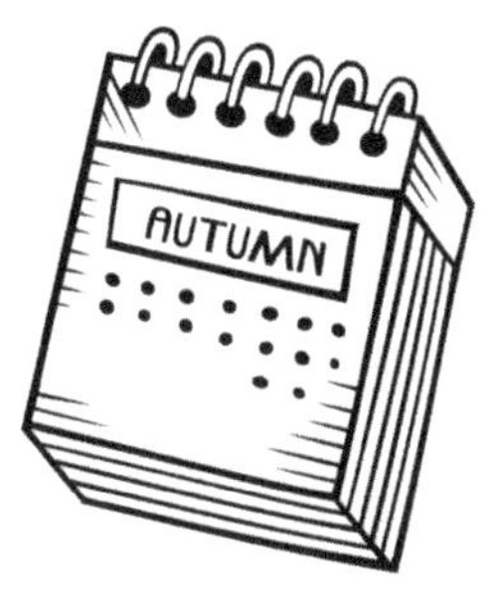

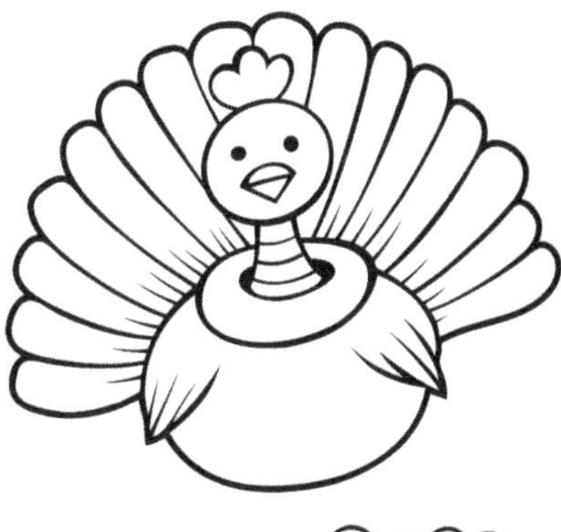

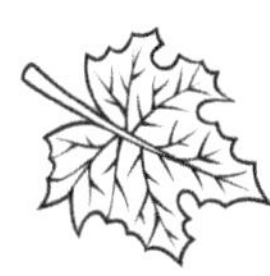

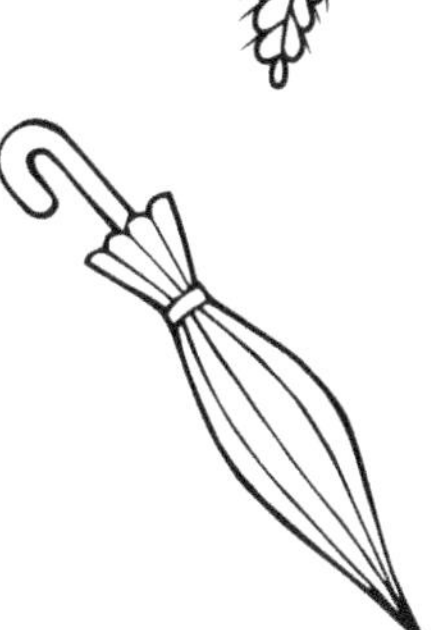

November

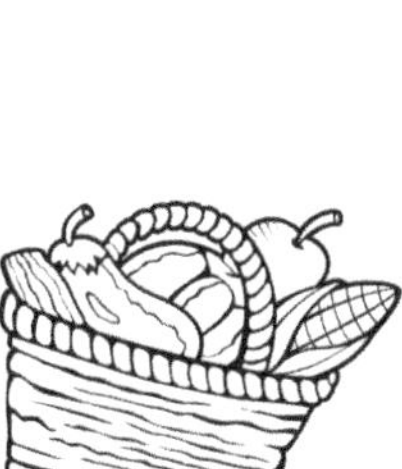

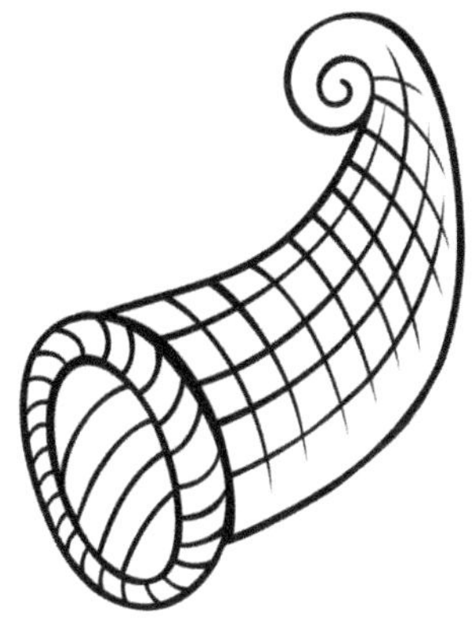

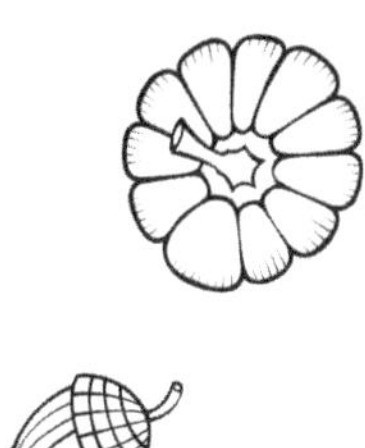

Happy people
continuously change,
and because
they change
they become
more and more happy
and then more and
more change
is possible.

~ Osho

November

Week of

Sunday

Monday

Tuesday

Wednesday

Thursday

Friday

Saturday

Write It Out...

- 3 things I am thankful for
- 5 ways I cans show my gratitude

November

Week of

Sunday

Monday

Tuesday

Wednesday

Thursday

Friday

Saturday

Mindful Reflection

Truly Taste

Take some time during your meals this month to breathe in the scent of the foods that are on the table.

Reflect on the makers of the food from growing the various vegetables and fruits to the cook who put all the ingredients together to create the aroma.

Chew slowly taking in the flavors with each bite. Try to identify as many spices as you can.

November

Week of

Sunday

Monday

Tuesday

Wednesday

Thursday

Friday

Saturday

Mak er Moment

Create a Centerpiece of Thankfulness

- ◊ Collect cardboard, recyled plastic bottles, glass jars, caps, containers
- ◊ Tape, glue, any adhesive
- ◊ Paper (different colors) or Tissue Paper
- ◊ Twigs, branches, pinecones, other natural dryed material
- ◊ Acrylic Paint /Brushes

#givemebackmycrayonsNovember

November

Week of

Sunday

Monday

Tuesday

Wednesday

Thursday

Friday

Saturday

Photo / Artwork Picture

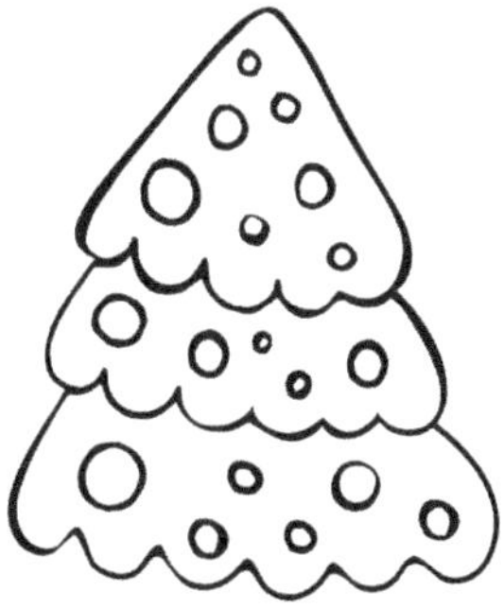

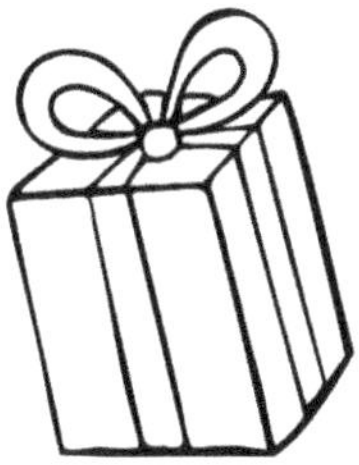

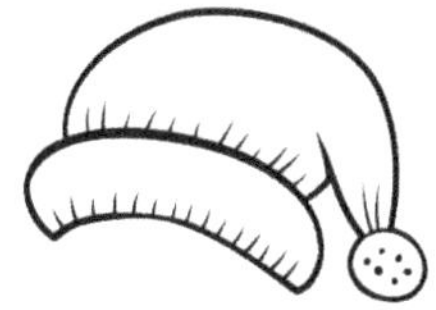

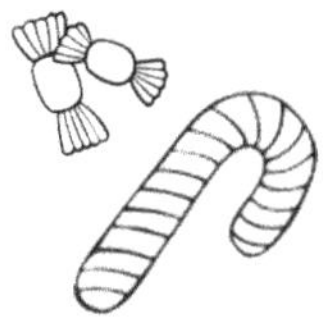

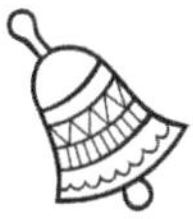

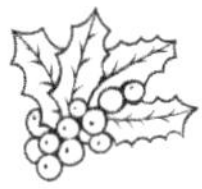

December

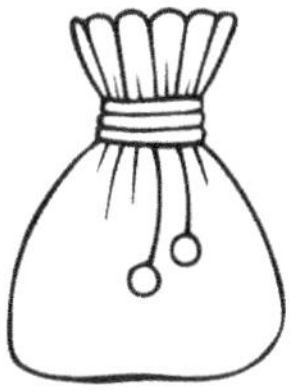

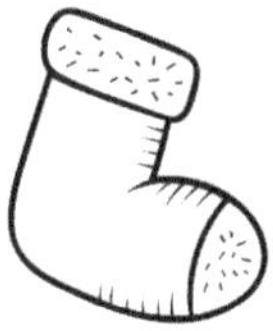

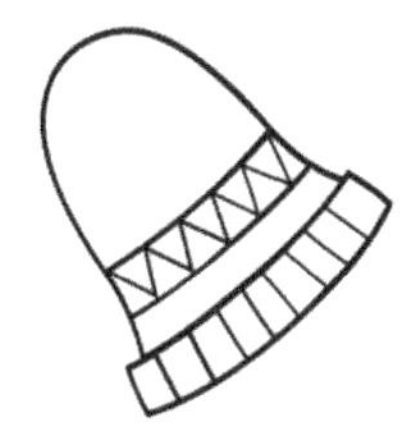

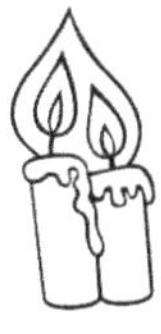

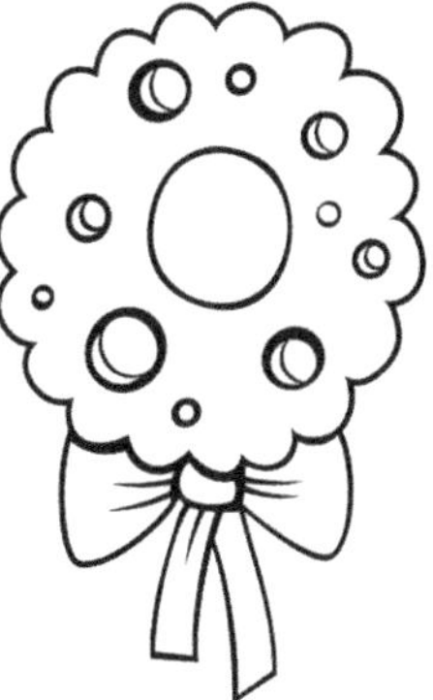

Love is what we were born with.
Fear is what we learn.
The spiritual journey is the unlearning
of fear and prejudices and the acceptance
of love back in our hearts. Love is the
essential reality and our purpose
on Earth. To be consciously aware of it,
to experience love in ourselves and others,
is the meaning of life. Meaning does not
lie in things. Meaning lies in us.

~ Marianne Williamson

December

Week of ____________

Sunday

Monday

Tuesday

Wednesday

Thursday

Friday

Saturday

Write It Out...

My favorite chidlhood memory of a holiday gathering...

My family kept this holiday tradition...

December

Week of

Sunday

Monday

Tuesday

Wednesday

Thursday

Friday

Saturday

Mindful Reflection

Remember to BREATHE...

During the busy times around the holidays we forget to take time to nourish ourselves with self-care. Find quiet time to just sit and breathe. Take in the sights, sounds, smells of the hustle-bustle.

Breathe in and out five times to relax your mind and body.

December

Week of

Sunday

Monday

Tuesday

Wednesday

Thursday

Friday

Saturday

Maker Moment

Postcard

Find a postcard from your hometown. If tourists were visiting your town during the holidays, what would you want them to see and feel from your creativity.

Create your own version of a postcard during the holidays that you imagine being displayed in a shop where tourists visit.

Postcard:

#givemebackmycrayonsDecember

December

Week of

Sunday

Monday

Tuesday

Wednesday

Thursday

Friday

Saturday

Photo / Artwork Picture

www.ingramcontent.com/pod-product-compliance
Lightning Source LLC
LaVergne TN
LVHW010951100826
845153LV00002B/195

* 9 7 8 0 5 7 8 6 8 8 3 0 5 *